★ ★ ★ ⭐

Hillary's MEDICAL DICTIONARY

★ ★ ★ ★ ★ ★ ★ ★ ★ ★ ★ ★ ★

by

Carl R. Krigbaum

Illustrations by Steve Parker

EVVI PUBLISHING

Cover and text illustrations by Steve Parker

SOURCE BOOKS
Dorland's *Illustrated Medical Dictionary*
Reader's Digest — *Family Health Guide*
Richard Wagman, M. D. — *Medical and Health Encyclopedia*

ISBN #0-9640776-0-4

Printed in the United States of America

Copyright ©1994 by Carl R. Krigbaum. All rights reserved. This book or any portion thereof may not be reproduced in any form, except for review purposes, without the written permission of the author.

Information in this book is deemed to be authentic and accurate by the author. However, he disclaims any liability incurred in connection with the use of information appearing in this book.

EVVI Publishing
P.O. Box 277
Page, AZ 86040

Table of Contents

To the Reader 4
A — *Abortion* to *Autosite* 5
B — *Back pain* to *Buccal* 7
　　Bunion to *Bypass* 8
C — *Caesarean section* to *Centigrade* 9
　　Central nervous system to *Coughin'* 11
　　Crabs to *Cyclamates* 12
D — *D & C* to *Dumdum fever* 14
E — *Eating habits* to *Eye wash* 15
F — *Face-bow* to *Fundus* 16
G — *Gangrene* to *Gyre* 17
H — *Habit* to *Heating Pad* 19
　　Heels to *Hirsute* 20
　　Hives to *Hysteria* 21
I — *Impotent* to *Isolate* 22
J-K　*Jaws* to *Kukuruku* 23
L — *Labor pains* to *Lytta* 25
M — *Malady* to *MRI* 27
　　Morbid to *Mycete* 28
N — *Narry* to *Nyxis* 29
O — *Occlusion* to *Oxide* 31
P — *Pacemaker* to *Pharynx* 33
　　Phlebitis to *Polyp* 34
　　Ponograph to *Pyrexia* 35
Q — *Quack* to *Rhythm method* 37
R — *Rib* to *Rutin* 38
S — *Saccular* to *Shingles* 39
　　Shock to *Stretcher* 41
　　Stupe to *Systole* 42
T — *Tablet* to *Transvestite* 43
　　Tremor to *Turbinate* 44
U-V　*Udder* to *Vulcanite* 45
W-Z　*Warbles* to *Zoospore* 46
Meet the Author 47

To the Reader

Would you hire a carpenter to work on your car? Or a sanitary engineer to fix your microwave? No? Then, like me, you probably wouldn't want a politician doing your brain surgery!

Alas, though, since Hillary Rodham Clinton has taken such an avid interest in health care reform for the country, we now face a new crisis: whether she and her political angels of mercy really know what they're talking about as they so glibly utilize the verbiage of the medical profession on radio and television.

So . . . with Mr. and Mrs. Average Citizen in mind, this author did weeks of cloak-and-dagger snooping in the White House and Congressional buildings, eavesdropping on countless conversations at important cocktail parties (to which he was not invited), then culminating it all by regularly listening to the Rush Limbaugh show.

Here is my conclusion:
> *THEY HAVEN'T THE FOGGIEST!*

So, it became necessary for me to painstakingly log all of their terminology, decipher what they thought it meant, and pass it on to you in this new medical dictionary.

Should you become sick (heaven forbid), at least you can now look up the term and figure out what kind of help you'll receive from Washington, D. C., when they hear of your illness.

I hope you have as much fun reading this as I have had in putting it together for you!

Carl R. Krigbaum

— A —

Abortion	Fickle sow shuns former boar-friend
Abrade	Hairstyle for ladies
Acetum	An usher's job
Achy	What you unlock door with
Acinous cell	Incarcerated donkey
Acoustic	What you shoot pool with
Adduct	Farm bird that goes "quack"
Adhere	Place where you figure the sum (total)
Adulthood	A grown-up thug
Afferent	Landlord comes for it the 1st of month
Afterbirth	Period of time after having baby
Agar	Vicious river fish with lots of teeth
Agenesis	First book of the Bible
Antabuse	Slapping Daddy's sister around
Anthrone	Where the king sits
Antigen	Nickname for Aunt Jennifer
Aphonia	What you a-talkie into
Artery	Where art objects are kept
Asian flu	Oriental goes by jet
Athletic supporter	Football fan
Atrium	Clinton paid $200 for one in LA airport
Auricle	Item in a newspaper
Autistic	Has a flair for art
Autograft	Request to sign name
Autosite	Used car lot

— Hillary's Medical Dictionary —

— B —

Back pain	Rear window
Bacteria	Rear door of a cafeteria
Balance	What Congress can't do to budget
Ball & socket joint	Wheel alignment shop
Barium	What morticians do
Bear down technique	Smokey retires for the night
Bends	A stretching exercise
Benign	A bingo number
Benzyl	Ben took sick
Belly button	Billy goat hits you in stomach
Beri-beri	Two pieces of fruit
Bile duct	A way to cook a fowl
Birth injury	Falling from Pullman sleeper
Birth rate	Cost of ticket for Pullman sleeper
Bleeding	A tactic used by I.R.S.
Blind spot	A dog that can't see
Blue baby	A sad little fella
Body scanner	Lecherous old goat
Boil	Method of cooking
Bowel	A-E-I-O-U
Breaking out	Inmates get loose
Bridge	Card game
Broncho pneumonia	A disease of horses
Broncho-scope	Mouthwash for horses
Brows	Looking but not buying
Buccal	The fastener at the end of your belt

— Hillary's Medical Dictionary —

— B —

Bunion   A big man with an axe
Bust   Police raid
Busted leg   Leg with a bust growing out of it
Bypass   A different route during construction

BRONCHO-SCOPE

– C –

Caesarean section	A neighborhood in Rome
Caffeine	A female calf
Calculus	College arithmetic
Calf	A baby cow
Callus	Hard, uncaring attitude
Cancellate	Calling regrets after party is over
Caput	Ruined—done in
Carbuncle	Part of a seatbelt
Carcinoid	Which means it probably won't start
Carotid	Car is all rusted out
Carpal	Persons who share driving to work
Cast	Actors in a play
Casting	Work done in a foundry
Cat scan	Looking at a kitty
Cataract	A big fancy car by GM
Catarrh	What Roy Clark plays
Caudad	Old song—"You git a line & I'll get a pole"
Cauterize	Made eye contact with a girl
Cautery	A corded twill material
Celibate	Honoring important event with big party
Cell bridge	Card game for inmates
Centigrade	Mailed a college score

— Hillary's Medical Dictionary —

– C –

Central nervous system	The U. S. Congress
Chest	Cedar box to put linens in
Childhood	A young thug
Cholera	To put on a dog's neck
Choline	Irish lass
Chorea	Far East country
Clasp (medical)	Medical personnel embracing
Cleaning agent	Something like a maid
Clinical death	Patient expires after long wait in clinic
Club foot	Son of Bigfoot
Codeine	Assistant to head of college
Cold medicine	It's kept in the refrigerator
Cold turkey	Thanksgiving entree
Colic	A popular breed of dog
Coma	A punctuation mark
Condom	A successful scam
Consumption	Act of eating
Contusion	State of Congress while in session
Conversion	The way the inmate told it
Conversion hysteria	Joining church while on emotional high
Corn	A joke from Arkansas
Corns	Two jokes from Arkansas
Coroner	Where two walls meet
Cortin	Boy and girl on date
Coughin'	What they bury you in

— Hillary's Medical Dictionary —

– C –

Crabs — Couple of nasty old people
Cramps — What you call Grandpa
Crick — Flows down the holler
Cross eye — An orb that is out of sorts
Croup — Smaller than a sedan
Crown — What the Queen wears on her head
Culture — Way of life of ethnic group
Cyclamates — Two on a motorcycle

— Hillary's Medical Dictionary —

– D –

D & C	Where White House is
Dagga	A small curved knife
Decaffeinated	Cow has abortion
Debridement	Divorce
Depression	Bad times in 1929-30
Diagnostic	One who dies, still not believing in God
Dilate	Live longer than average
Dilator	Haven't got time to expire right now
Discharge	Running down the battery
Discission	Made up my mind
Disk	A farm implement
Dislocation	Right here is the spot
Doctor	Withheld some of her pay
Doctor's invoice	The physician is ready to sing
Dominant	One who plays dominoes
Dope	Dumbbell—idiot
Down syndrome	A goose with sick feathers
Dressing	A food that goes with turkey
Dropsy	Tide goes out
Dry socket	What mechanics do when socket gets wet
Dumdum fever	Prevalent in Washington, D.C.

— Hillary's Medical Dictionary —

– E –

Eating habits	What nuns wear to dinner
Egg cell	High scorer, one who does very well
Elective surgery	Doctors vote on whether to operate
Enema	Not a friend
Endoblast	Dynamite all used up
Endoscope	Scope is dropped on floor
Erection	Putting up a building
Eruption	Volcanic action
Ester	Book in the Old Testament
Ether	One or the other
Eucrasia	Hey, man! You're nuts!
Exon shuffle	Shake-up in gasoline industry
Expectorate	The speed measurement of spitting
Eyestrain	Sees a locomotive
Exudate	Taking out your ex-wife
Eye wash	It's time for my bath

— Hillary's Medical Dictionary —

– F –

Face-bow	What William Tell's son did
Facelift	Vicious uppercut to the jaw
Fallen arches	Two men, both named Arch, collide and fall down
Family-practice Dr.	Physician who uses your family as guinea pigs
Fat pad	Where obese people live
Fester	Quicker
Fetography	Taking pictures
Fissure	One who goes fishing
Flare-up	Warning signal goes skyward
Flat-foot	Walking policeman
Foramen	Man in charge of workers
Foreplay	Two couples go bowling
Fraise	What worn collars and cuffs do
Fretum	Like "fretum of speech," etc.
Fundus	Lobbyist's most used phrase

— Hillary's Medical Dictionary —

— G —

Gangrene	Color worn by certain street gangs
Genes	Denim pants
Genital	Anyone not Jewish
Germicide	Mass suicide of germs
G. I. series	Championship game for veterans
Globulin	Popular at Halloween parties
Glucan	What you store glue in
Goiter	Elastic band to hold up your socks
Grand Mal	Big shopping center
Grippe	Firm handshake
Grub	Vittles
Gum	Something you chew
Gurneys	A breed of milk cow
Gut feeling	What surgeon does inside your tummy
Gypsum	"You can fool some of the people," etc.
Gyre	What you can fruit in

— Hillary's Medical Dictionary —

— H —

Habit	Something a nun wears
Haff disease	You're partly sick
Hair dye	What causes baldness
Hair loss	Theft of rabbit
Hammertoe	Carpenter misses nail—hits foot
Hand piece	Saturday night special
Hangnail	Coat hook
Hangover	Didn't break neck first time
Hare lip	Part of rabbit's mouth
Hatter's disease	Common ailment for lady in millinery shoppe
Head	Bathroom
Heart	A male red deer
Heart blocks	What doctor's kids play with
Heating pad	Hippie warming up his room

HARELIP

— Hillary's Medical Dictionary —

— H —

Heels	First and last slices of bread
Helix	What friendly dog does when you pet him
Hemad	Man is angry
Heroin	Heroic female, i.e., Dr. Jocelyn Elders
Herpes	Found in lady's garden, with beans, carrots, etc.
Hiant	Greeting to daddy's sister
Hiccups	Drinking vessels for hillbillies
Hip	Up with it—real cool
Hip joint	A real swinging dive
Hipshot	Worn out—needs joint replacement
Hirsute	Lady's bridge-hand

— Hillary's Medical Dictionary —

— H —

Hives	What you keep bees in
Hock	Put up item for collateral
Homograft	Extortion of gay people
Horn	Warning device on car
Hospital ward	Where patients hold caucuses
Humerus	Funny
Hunchback	Car with lift-up door in back
Hyaline	Overhead power line
Hyde's disease	Conceals symptoms
Hydrops	Skydiving at excessive altitudes
Hygiene	How you greet Mr. Autry
Hymen	Greeting a group of men
Hysteria	A purple creeping vine

— Hillary's Medical Dictionary —

– I –

Impotent	State of prominence, very significant
Incest	Emphatically demand
Incisor	Having a fit
Incus	Tribe in Peru
Indican	Where you throw de garbage
In labor	At work
Inoperable	Car won't run
Inose	Where your hay fever is
Insane	Fish caught in net
Insanity	Not sterile
Insight	Now is in view
Insulin	Stuff in attic and walls to keep cold out
Insultus	You make rude remarks to us
Intern	Take a number and wait
Intestine flu	Oops! Knife slips, part of gut sails away
Iodum	That's why I had to pay 'em
Iris	Pretty purple flower
Islet	What you put shoelace into
Isolate	Sorry I'm not on time

— Hillary's Medical Dictionary —

— J —

Jaws	A popular movie
Jerk	A nerd
Joint	Beer hall
Joule	Precious stone
Justo major	Next step is colonel

— K —

Kenalog	A roster of dogs kept in boarding by vet
Keratome	Family provides needed medical care in their house
Keratose	Medical expertise for ped digits
Kerion	Small luggage the airline allows with patron
Kernel	An officer in the Army
Kidney	A child's knee
Kink	Ruler of a country
Kilonem	What a fatal disease is doing
Knee jerk	A crummy doctor who works on knees
Kukuruku	Rooster's wake-up call

— Hillary's Medical Dictionary —

– L –

Labor pains	Getting hurt on the job
Labrale	Reading method for blind Frenchmen
Lac	Minus
Lactone	Singer not too hot
Lactose	Born without foot digits
Lance	Medieval weapon
Lap	How cats and dogs drink
Larynx	A big wildcat
Laughing gas	Expulsion of body gas posteriorly, causing laughter
Leech	Moocher
Lema	City in Ohio
Ligament	Medicine you rub on sore muscle
Ligation	A legal matter
Limb	Branch of a tree
Lisping	Boat is lower in water on one side
Litter	Bunch of new kitties or puppies
Liver	One who does not die
Lobite	Nip by a short dog
Loop	Area in Chicago
Louse	A nasty person
Lumbar	Used in building a house
Lymph	Favoring one leg while walking
Lyse	Falsehoods
Lytta	Trash

— Hillary's Medical Dictionary —

— Hillary's Medical Dictionary —

– M –

Malady	Tune of a song
Male	You get it at post office
Mammogram	Telegram for Mammy
Mandrels	Singing sisters from Grand Ole Opry
Manna	Method
Mass hysteria	Worshipers go bonkers
Matrass	You put it on a bed
Medical staff	Infection medical personnel get
Medicine dropper	Clumsy pharmacist
Meletin	Turning to liquid
Menarche	A breed of chicken
Menopause	Men stop working momentarily
Mercurochrome	Metal strips on a Mercury
Mesad	I'm unhappy
Metacele	Happened at Sea World
Micro	Pet raven
Microbe	A night garment for Mike
Migraine	Oats, wheat, corn, etc.
Migraine headache	Crop failure
Mock up	Margin of profit
Moles	Burrowing animals
Monaster	Horrible beast
Moner	One who complains a lot
Monkey paw	A daddy monkey
Moron	Adding more clothes
MRI	Bad English. Should say "him or me"

— Hillary's Medical Dictionary —

– M –

Morbid	A higher offer
Morrow	Day after today
Motor function	How well the car runs
Multi cell	Jail with more than one room
Mycete	Where I sit

– N –

Narry	None at all
Nasal drip	A nerd with a nose problem
Natolone	Not by myself
Navel	Pertaining to the Navy
Neck	You do it in the back seat
Needle	To taunt or jibe
Nerve	Unmitigated gall
Nerve ending	Election time is close
Nightmare	Lady horse of ill repute
Nihilism	Complete destruction
Nitrates	Lower than day rates
Niter	Nocturnal person
Nitride	Made famous by Paul Revere
Node	Knew about it
Nodus	Patient recognized everybody when he woke up
Nonose	Without proboscis
Nosepiece	Prosthesis for "nonose" patient
Nose drops	Embarrassing moment during rhinoplasty
Nyxis	Barber cuts us during shave

— Hillary's Medical Dictionary —

— O —

Occlusion	I've reached a decision
Off balance	U. S. Budget
Olfactory	Outdated assembly plant
Operative	A detective
Opiate	What Sheriff Andy Taylor's son did at supper time
Oral	Rev. Robert's first name
Orf	Dog talk
Organ donor	Benefactor of church instrument
Orifice	Where I go to work
Os	Land where the wizard lives
Osmatic	Has asthma
Ossicle	Tapered mass of ice hanging from roof in winter
Otophone	Telephone in car
Out patient	Patient who has fainted
Ova	Done with
Ovaries	How you like your eggs cooked
Overbite	Recovered from the attack
Overweight	Time spent in Dr.'s waiting room
Oxide	Skin of an ox

— Hillary's Medical Dictionary —

– P –

Pacemaker	Diplomat
Pain	Glass window
Palate	First name was Pontius
Panostitis	Disease of extreme pain in right side
Pancreas	Long dent in a pan
Pap smear	Attempt to slander your Daddy
Pap test	Test for fatherhood
Papulation	Number of people in given area
Paradox	Two doctors
Paralyze	Two untruths
Parasites	Two different locations
Parrot fever	The bird is a little hot
Paster	Preacher
Pastern	Where preacher lives
Pasteur treatment	Putting old folks out to graze— Euthanasia is next
Pedophile	Use it to sand down your toenails
Peeping tom	A perverted turkey
Pelvis	Cousin to Elvis
Penile	Do not do in the river in Egypt
Peptonic	Something like Hadacol
Period	Another punctuation mark
Periotic	Regularly
Peyote	Cousin to coyote
Pharynx	City in Arizona

— Hillary's Medical Dictionary —

– P –

Phlebitis	What insect does to us in swamp
Phonomania	Teenage illness
Phylum	What you do to your fingernails
Pigeon-toed	Cross between bird and frog
Piles	Stacks of something or other
Pill box	Cute little hat
Pinch test	Romantic tweak of fingers in drive-in
(black eye)	Results of pinch test
Plaque	Award you hang on wall
Pleural	More than one
Plug	An old horse
Pock	You play hockey with it
Polkissen	Politician & babies near election time
Polyp	Sound made by bag of water hitting floor

— Hillary's Medical Dictionary —

– P –

Ponograph	Record-player
Pontiac fever	Urge to buy new car
Pore	Without funds
Pork (under-cooked)	In Washington, DC, where it is over-cooked, it causes headache
Post-operative	A letter carrier
Posture	Where cows graze
Potts disease	Self explanatory; sometimes called "trots"
Pressor	Worker in dry cleaners
Prostate	Flat on the ground
Protein	In favor of teenagers
Proal	Letting convicts out early
Prunin	Trimming your bushes
Psychedelic drug	Colorful person caught in bumper of moving car
Psychoanalyst	Analyst who is nuts
Psychosis	Your nutty sister
Pulmotor	What mechanic does to busted block
Pulp	A baby dog
Pupil	A student
Pygal	Lady who works in bakery
Pyknosis	A nasty repugnant habit
Pylon	A no-no in football
Pyrexia	A good type of bake ware

— Hillary's Medical Dictionary —

— Q —

Quack	Duck talk
Quackery	2nd rate clinic that hires medical rejects
Quinsy	A city in Illinois

— R —

Race	A speed contest
Radical surgery	Operating on a far-left or far-right politician
Radio plastic	A cheap little unit
Rage	Latest fad
Rale	What a train travels on
Rash	Action with little thought
Recess	Popular play-time at school
Recovery room	A place to do upholstery
Rectoscope	Ruined it
Rectum	Dang near killed 'em, too!
Redox	A colorful animal
Refraction	Figuring your algebra over
Remission	Patient returns to hospital
Renal calculus	Medical arithmetic
Resection	Did the land-survey wrong the first time
Rest	All that's left
Retrad	Recapping an old tire
Rhubarb	Fight at a ball game
Rhythm method	A piano technique

— Hillary's Medical Dictionary —

– R –

Rib — Taunt or jibe
Ribs — A restaurant delicacy
Rotz — Decays
Roughage — After you hit forty
Rupture — Great event when Christians leave Earth
Rutin — Hogs do it—so do sports fans

– S –

Saccular	Non-religious
Sacred	Religious
Sane	What you catch fish with
Sap	Not too bright a person
Scab	Not popular with labor unions
Scaler	One who climbs mountains
Scalp	Selling tickets at exorbitant prices
Scoop	A hot news story
Seasickness	Observing one who is ill
Sebum	Observes a hobo
Secondary	In case one dairy is insufficient
Seizure	Roman emperor
Self denial	Nope, it ain't me
Sellar	Basement
Sense organs	Not prevalent in Washington, D.C.
Senile	Gazing at river in Egypt
Semen	Observing the male gender
Septic shock	When stool overflows
Serfin	Fun on a surfboard
Serum	Burning a patient
Sexual drive	Trip to lovers' lane
Sexual identity	When doctor tells you if it's a boy or girl
Sexual intercourse	Two persons discussing sex
Shaking palsy	Getting rid of it
Shingles	What you roof your house with

— Hillary's Medical Dictionary —

– S –

Shock	Part of car's suspension system
Shot	Gunfire
Silicon	Nutty inmate
Sinusal	We'll all enlist together
Skin graft	Black market for skin
Slipped disc	A pilfered album
Sole	An edible fish
Spanish fly	Zipper in a pair of Mexican pants
Sperm cell	Where naughty sperm is confined
Sphincter	Found in the pyramids
Spine	Splinter from a cactus
Sprain	Follows winter
Stable	Where horses are kept
Staph infection	What doctors get
Stage	Where actors perform
Static	Interference on radio
Stenosis	Sister is a secretary
Steroid	One hooked on stereo
Stiffness	Over-formal and distant
Sting	A covert operation
Strangulation	A felony, if fatal
Streak	Popular naked run a few years back
Stripping (vein)	An arrogant burlesque queen at work
Stroke	Petting a kitty
Stool	Something you sit on
Stretcher	Device to make you taller

— Hillary's Medical Dictionary —

– S –

Stupe	Idiot, fool
St. Vitus dance	A Catholic social event
Support hose	Hose hanger
Swallowing	Part of the swallow that allows it to fly
Sycosis	Sister has mental problem
Symphyses	Musical program
Synapsis	Brief description
Syndrome	Building where you can commit evil deeds
Systole	Your klepto sister lifted an item

— T —

Tablet	A small table
Tachy	Tasteless—out of place
Tail	Someone following you
Tampon	Something you do to a pile of dirt
Tarsal	Hangs on graduate's mortar-board
Taxis	Popular plaything with Congress
Taxon	Adds to
Teething	A thing you make tea in
Temple	Place of worship
Tension	Command from drill sergeant
Terminal illness	Getting sick at the airport
Testes	Ones who take tests (from testors)
Testicle	A test done by tickling the patient
Texis	Where Alamo is
Thermogram	A hot-to-trot Grandma
Thorax	Large surgical blade
Thrush	A bird
Tic	Nasty little bug
Tiring	Replacing tires
Toe	To pull a vehicle
Tooth fairy	A gay dentist
Tourniquet	Banquets given at end of tournament
Tracer	A genealogist
Trachoma	City in Washington state
Tract	Followed a set of footprints
Transvestite	A gay who's had too much to drink

— Hillary's Medical Dictionary —

– T –

Tremor	Garden tool to trim hedge with
Triangle	Hopeless love situation
Trench mouth	Open end of a ditch
Truss	Congress has hard time finding any these days
Trypsin	Nonchalantly skips into the house
Tussal	Scuffle
Tumor	A couple extra
Turbinate	End of it—get rid of him!

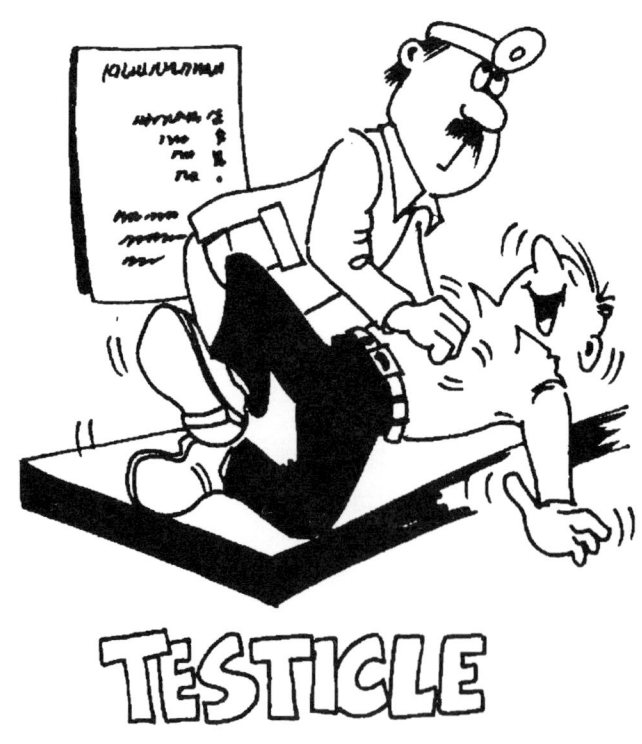

TESTICLE

— Hillary's Medical Dictionary —

– U –

Udder	Making sound
Underhorn	Is where you find the cow, goat, etc.
Union	Powerful labor force
Urate	Yes, sir! You *are* special!
Urine	You are now a member
Uronophile	We've got your record
Urosis	Flowers in your yard

– V –

Vagus	City in Nevada
Valence	Top curtain
Varicole	Chilled to the bone
Varicose	Nearby
Vastest	Speediest
Vault	Catapulting
Vector	One who wins
Veil	Ski resort in Colorado
Vein	Arrogant—proud
Venous	Far away planet
Vice	A clamping tool
Vital signs	Like "stop," "men working," "yield," etc.
Voice box	Verbal sparring
Void	Stay away from
Vulcanite	What Mr. Spock is

— Hillary's Medical Dictionary —

— W —

Warbles — Attempts to sing
Wash — Sandy ravine without water
Waxing — Doing the floors
Weight — Hold on for a minute
Wheel — Car has four of them
Withdrawal — Taking money out of the bank

— X —

Xenia — Pretty little flower
Xero — Nothing
Xylo — To store grain in

— Y —

Yawn — Put up or shut up! You've got a deal!
Yaws — One on each side of your face

— Z —

Zip — What you do with a zipper
Zoospore — Needs a donation

— Hillary's Medical Dictionary —

Meet the Author

Author with his "children", Brannie & Bronnie

Carl Krigbaum has loved both comedy and music all of his life. He has written and acted in many of his own comedies at school PTA's and community programs and copyrighted several of his musical compositions.

His "medical" background includes eight years at the Fort Whipple Veteran's Hospital (near Prescott, Arizona). As a young man, he aspired to be a veterinarian, but instead found work in Skull Valley where his uncle was a ranch foreman. He says "We did our own 'medical work' there, too, on horses and cattle alike. Sometimes I felt we could dismantle a cow and put her back together!"

Mr. Krigbaum's political know-how flourished when he worked with *The Arizona Republic* columnist Bill Nixon in quite a number of Arizona's version of Washington's political "Gridiron" show. He wrote part of their musical lampoons (words and music) as well as participating in the productions.

A life-long registered Democrat who has never missed a chance to exercise his vote, Mr. Krigbaum is retired and lives in Page, Arizona.

ORDER FORM

To order additional copies of **Hillary's Medical Dictionary**, please complete and mail the following:

I would like to order _____ copies @ $3.95 per copy

My check/money order is enclosed for: _____
(Please include $2.00 shipping per order.)

_____
Name

_____
Telephone No.   Apt. No.

_____
Address

_____
City

_____
State   Zip

Mail order form to: **EVVI Publishing**
                          P.O. Box 277
                          Page, AZ 86040

For Quantity Discounts, write to Publisher

(This form may be photo-copied)